# *oriental*
# CRAFT PAINTING

## by Pauline Cherrett

ISBN 1 871517 30 3

## Osmiroid Creative Leisure Series

# About the Author

Pauline Cherrett, an Architect with the NHS, was fascinated from childhood by anything oriental. The concepts of space were absorbed from Ikebana (Japanese Flower Arranging). Ten years ago Pauline was introduced to Chinese Brush Painting by Jean Long and has since studied with several different teachers, including the Chinese artist whose work appears in this book. After obtaining the Stage 1 Adult Education Certificate in Chinese Brush Painting, she started teaching in Hampshire and other parts of the country. Her design work in other fields is also influenced by Chinese Brush Painting. She is a founder member and the Secretary of the Chinese Brush Painters Society, and has promoted the art of Chinese Brush Painting with demonstrations/talks for exhibitions, shows and clubs. Her first Osmiroid book, "Chinese Brush Painting", was primarily for beginners. In this, the second book, she explores the use of different surfaces for decoration in this painting style and shows the versatility of both the strokes and the brushes.

# CONTENTS

# INTRODUCTION

Chinese Brush Painting is a fascinating art form which originated hundreds of years ago. It has many traditional aspects, and is mainly carried out using special brushes and inks, painting onto paper or silk.

The whole essence of the art is to portray a subject, not in botanical or anatomical detail, but almost in cartoon or caricature form showing only the main features for recognition. This results in a style where the beauty of the brush strokes can be appreciated, and where the space surrounding the design is as important as the subject itself.

This book illustrates some of the uses to which your paintings can be put, other than the purely decorative, framed or mounted picture.

There are many examples, together with instructions. The book intends to give ideas and, hopefully, to promote thoughts for additional and different applications.

*Pandas by Qu Lei Lei*

# ABOUT CHINESE BRUSH PAINTING

This chapter sets out to explain the main points and the method of painting in the Chinese style. The primary concern is about space.

The Oriental concept of space is something to which the Westerner has to become accustomed. This is done by examining the paintings of the 'Masters' and by absorbing the various features from crafts, photographs and illustrations.

The most important items of equipment when using the Chinese Brush Painting traditions for uses other than painting on paper are the brushes. These are very different to any others and hold far more liquid. For small items of work it is obviously not necessary to have large brushes. The surface to be painted on should be absorbent. In the first instance it is best to practise on Chinese painting paper until you feel confident enough to try other surfaces.

In this book the main emphasis is on alternative uses for the painting, so it is assumed that watercolours (either Western or Oriental varieties) and specialist paints will be the main mediums rather than the inks more commonly used.

For those who have not tried this art form the following steps should be followed. A suitable workspace should be found, with adequate light, room to move, and a good working-height seat and work surface. The paper should be held down with weights, and two waterpots will be required (one for 'clean colours' and the other for colours containing black), together with some watercolour paints. If new brushes are being used the starch protection should be washed out in cold or lukewarm water. The protecting covers should never be replaced after this stage.

*Each flower petal is carried out as a separate stroke, these are arranged to give a flower shape. The heel of the brush is moved sideways, the tip staying still. By varying the size of the petals the flower can be made to look in a specific direction. The brush is loaded with colour, with a darker one on the tip. When the tip of the brush is placed into the centre of the flower, this gives the effect shown. The stamens are added when petals are dry.*

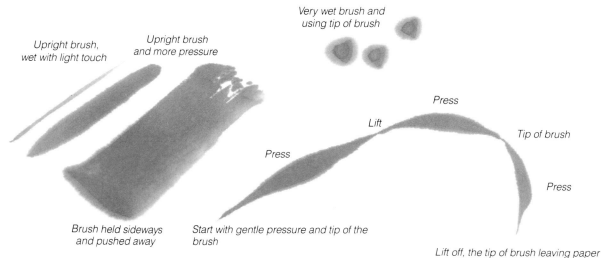

*Upright brush, wet with light touch*

*Upright brush and more pressure*

*Very wet brush and using tip of brush*

*Press*

*Lift*

*Press*

*Tip of brush*

*Press*

*Brush held sideways and pushed away*

*Start with gentle pressure and tip of the brush*

*Lift off, the tip of brush leaving paper with a flicking movement*

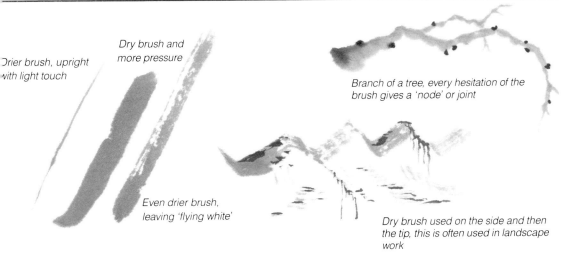

Drier brush, upright with light touch

Dry brush and more pressure

Branch of a tree, every hesitation of the brush gives a 'node' or joint

Even drier brush, leaving 'flying white'

Dry brush used on the side and then the tip, this is often used in landscape work

Two examples of leaves, showing the small amount of stem that needs to be shown, and how the shape of each leaf can be varied by application of the veins. These veins should be applied when the leaves are nearly dry - if they are added too soon then the paint will run. 'Mi' dots are added to give a rougher branch.

Using a white/cream plate or palatte, the colour is loaded onto the prepared brush. In order to increase the interest in your brush strokes, the brush can be loaded with more than one colour. Try putting two or three colours onto the brush, working progressively towards the tip. Another technique is to load the brush with a colour mixed in the palette, and then to dip the tip into one of the colours just before the stroke is made. The illustrations show this in more detail.

Flowers should be shown in their natural colours, adding some black to the leaf colours. Flower petals should not contain any black, although detail such as stamens may. All your paintings should contain *'life'*. This is helped by observation: how a leaf or flower is joined to a stem, how many petals there are, the style of the stamens and other such detail will make your work believable.

Having assembled the colours and equipment, you should get used to varying the pressure of the brush and the amount of liquid necessary. You will find quite a contrast between a dry brush stroke, which leaves areas of white paper (indicating age and texture - an old branch of a tree), and a very wet, fluffy stroke (soft and furry - for animals). Practise adding water to the paint to vary the shades of colour, remembering to wipe the brush on the side of the plate or palatte to adjust the amount of liquid in the brush to the desired level. Experiment with some of the examples given in later chapters to try out the various types of strokes and subjects. Just as different papers are made with varying amounts of size which alter their absorbancy, so the different mediums dealt with in this book will vary.

There are many techniques used in traditional work, but the main two are solid and outline strokes. These are fairly descriptive of the way the strokes are painted.

*Examples of decorated notepaper, painted on handmade paper - rag, straw and old christmas cards included! The waterlily is shown with solid strokes, plum and hibiscus as a mixture of solid and outline, and the butterfly totally in outline strokes. By using homemade paper you can control the amount of size in the paper, and therefore the absorbency of it.*

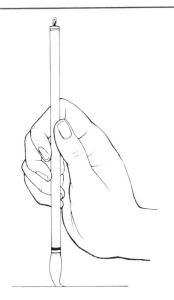

# Solid Strokes

Used for petals, leaves and branches, the brush is held rather like chopsticks, with the handle between the second and third fingers and the thumb supporting it on the other side. This allows a 'balanced' grip. If a petal or 'soft' stroke is required, the brush is held at an angle. When a strong or powerful stroke is needed, an upright brush is used. The palm of the hand should be hollow as though holding an egg. Try not to grip the brush too tightly, otherwise your brush strokes will be stilted.

The brush is loaded with a single colour or, if desired, two or three colours. The tip of the brush is then touched to the paper, moving the heel or the whole brush to obtain the width and length of stroke required. With Chinese brushes, the strokes can be made in any direction, pulling and pushing forward, backwards and sideways.

*he upright brush is used for strong*
*rokes i.e. stems and branches. Try not*
*) grip the brush too tightly. The wrist*
*nd fingers should be flexible.*

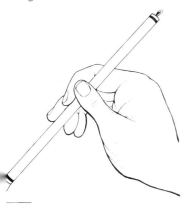

# Outline Strokes

These can be mixed with solid strokes. Plum blossom, for example, can have the petals in outline and the branches in solid. Orchids can have the same, with the flowers (being the more delicate part of the plant) in outline and the leaves in solid strokes. All outline is also permissible but does not have the same impact - it has been popular at various times during the many years of Chinese Brush Painting.

A fine brush is used for the outline strokes, which are almost drawn. The arm should be kept clear of the work surface, being free to move in any direction. If very fine, detailed work is being done, then the wrist only may rest down. The outline shape produced can be filled in with colour if desired, or can have a second line either inside or outside the original line in a lighter colour. The outer additional line is a more modern technique.

*he angled brush is used for the softer*
*rokes such as petals and leaves. The*
*and is further from the paper than with*
*ny Western art, to allow more*
*ovement of the brush. For larger work*
*tists sometimes hold the brush at the*
*p.*

# The Complete Painting

If a flower is your subject start with the petals, working round the flower, making sure that the blooms are facing in different directions. Next paint the leaves, taking care to arrange them so that they look natural and right for the plant - some will be stiff and spiky, others will be soft and flowing. The next stage is to paint in the stem or branch. If your leaves have been positioned naturally you will not usually see the stem in its entirety, but in spaces between the leaves. By hesitating along the length of the stem, the paint will soak in more and there will be natural nodes from which sideshoots can be painted.

Any veins that you wish to paint on the leaves should now be added. The leaf should neither be too dry, nor so wet that the paint runs into the leaf colour. Lastly, the stamens or pistils are added to the flowers - this is done when the petals are dry.

If a stroke is not right or the brush misses the paper slightly, do not go over that stroke again as it will always show, and your painting will lose its freshness and transparency.

Once you feel that you have some control over the pressure required, the amount of liquid and the direction that the brush needs to go, then you can progress to the next subject.

*Small paintings on silk acetate ribbon displayed in gilt or fabric frames.*

# CARDS AND BOOKMARKS

Small paintings for greetings cards and bookmarks are approached in the same way as larger paintings. The same principles of shape, space and colour apply. The main difference is in size.

It is very important to find the correct scale, and therefore the choice of subject. Unless you can paint in small detail, a landscape would need to be very simple. It is useful to be able to pick out a small area of a picture or scene; if too much is included the work looks crowded.

There are several types of card mount on the market, with varying designs of aperture. Square or rectangular are obviously better for landscapes or animals, while the daintiness of flowers or birds are set off by an oval or circle. The card size can vary from 75mm x 100mm to 150mm x 225mm (approximate sizes). Some are self-adhesive and others depend on the application of glue. Which you use will depend on availability and cost.

Another factor to be considered is the selection of card colour. White or cream will usually set off any design, whereas a coloured card will need a more dominant painting to avoid being overshadowed by the mount.

The choice of material for painting on will vary, influenced by personal taste, availability and what you are happy using. Paper can of course be used, together with silk, artificial silk ribbon or other suitable fabrics.

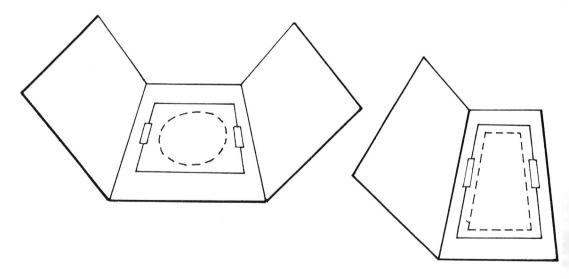

*Mounting work in a variety of card mounts*

# Painting on Silk or Other Fabrics

It will be necessary to ensure that you have the work flat, using coins or other weights. The other main contrast with painting on paper is that you will need a drier brush, otherwise the paint will follow the threads too much. Silk gives a delicate effect, especially if the colours are kept transparent by not being used too thickly.

If the work will not require washing, say for a card, then there is no need to use paints which withstand water - watercolours will be quite adequate. If washing is anticipated, then special paints will be needed. This is dealt with in a later chapter.

Do experiment both with paints and with different materials. Stiffened muslin or similar fabrics can be used successfully. When working with cards and other small items the amount of material required is very small of course. Investigation of the contents of boxes stored in the loft may well be rewarding!

*Animals and fish can be appealing or can add a touch of humour to cards. They can be sent to children, used for an appropriate situation, or just because the recipient has a fascination for the subject! The donkey and mice are both on paper, the fish on fabric.*

# Symbolism

When painting a card for a special occasion it is useful to consult a list of Chinese symbols. These can be found in many books but, for convenience, a list of some of the most useful is given below.

| | |
|---|---|
| **Affection** | Peony |
| **Approaching success** | Swallow |
| **Autumn** | Chrysanthemum, Olea fragrans, birds, butterflies |
| **Beauty** | Oleander, kingfisher, orchid, pheasant, peacock |
| **Bravery** | Bear, leopard |
| **Conjugal felicity** | Ducks, fish, butterflies, geese |
| **Courage** | Cricket, quail, tiger |
| **Creativity** | Lotus |
| **Energy** | Elephant, tiger, leopard, lion |
| **Eternal youth** | Cicada, crane |
| **Fair sex** | Apricots, azalea, cherry, willow, jasmine |
| **Fidelity** | Dog, lotus, parrot |
| **Filial piety** | Bamboo, dove, black crow |
| **Good fortune** | Pheasant, orange fruit, almond blossom, narcissus, peony |
| **Good omen** | Magpie |
| **Goodness** | Dragon |
| **Grace** | Oleander |
| **Happiness** | Bat, cicada |
| **Harmony** | Fish |
| **Health** | Monkey |
| **Hope** | Plum |
| **Immortality** | Cicada, orange fruit, fungus |
| **Joy** | Butterfly, persimmon |
| **Joviality** | Chrysanthemum |
| **Life** | Cock |
| **Longevity** | Bamboo, plum, fox, hare, crane, peach, deer, pine, carp |
| **Love** | Orchid, peony, convolvulus |
| **Marriage** | Goose, peach, convolvulus |
| **Mother of a family** | Day lily |

| | |
|---|---|
| **Numerous progeny** | Orchid |
| **Peace** | Apples, phoenix |
| **Perfect man** | Orchid |
| **Posterity** | Pomegranate |
| **Promotion** | Crane |
| **Prosperity** | Rat, phoenix |
| **Purity** | Lotus, plum |
| **Rain bringing** | Dragon |
| **Retired life** | Sheep, goat, palm |
| **Retirement** | Chrysanthemum |
| **Spring** | Tree peony, peach, willow, ox, cherry blossom, magnolia |
| **Strength** | Dragon, elephant, lion, bear |
| **Success** | Monkey |
| **Summer** | Butterfly, cricket, lotus, flags, pines, reeds |
| **Sweetness** | Jasmine, magnolia |
| **Warmth** | Cock |
| **Wealth** | Fish, Buddha's hand (citron) |
| **Winter** | Prunus, early roses, winter scenes |

This is not an exhaustive list and you will probably come across others. There are many more items with significant meanings but they would be more difficult to illustrate!

If you have taken care to choose your subject for a special card, a small note inserted inside or on the back indicating the meaning of the symbol would provide the finishing touch.

# Examples

### Rectangular aperture - portrait.

This shape is suitable for landscapes, flowers, animals, fish, birds and figures. You should ensure that there is enough space around the design to give the desired effect. This does not mean that you allow an equal border all round! What is required are different proportions of space, both to give breathing space and to add emphasis where necessary. This applies to any of the shapes and designs of course.

### Rectangular aperture - landscape.

With the horizontal, more care is necessary in choosing the appropriate painting. The example shown is a modern design, but more traditional subjects can be used. For instance, this shape will lend itself to a landscape, a branch or a spray of blossom. A fish or animal will also look well.

### Oval aperture.

This is very suitable for flowers and birds. The design needs to be of a suitable size and without too many 'stray' ends to be lost in the corners. For all designs, it is best to work with a piece of paper underneath with the aperture marked on it, so that your subject looks at its best. This obviously creates a restriction on size and shape, so your work should be carefully thought out beforehand.

*Various cards showing different subjects and mounts. The frogs are on paper, the rest are on silk acetate ribbon. Cards for birthdays or for Chinese New Year could illustrate the appropriate animal of the Chinese Zodiac. These feature in many astrology books. The seal used on the frog card is a pictogram of a sheep/goat. This seal and the others mentioned in the book have been carved by Qu Lei Lei.*

## Circular aperture.

This may be the most difficult one to deal with. The priority is to keep the design simple and rounded in shape.

*Small items such as jewellery and keyrings can be made. Bamboo paper was used for the keyring which is also double-sided.*

*The plastic compacts have been painted with Osmiroid Craft Colours. The paint needs to be dry before adding detail such as feathers and stamens.*

Calligraphy - Happy New Year and Happy Christmas in four styles (choose the style to suit your painting)
1 - standard, 2 - cursive, 3 - Han official, 4 - Qin Zhuan (ancient). All the four styles have been translated and painted by Qu Lei Lei.

Happy New Year

2

3

4

Happy Christmas

1

2

3

4

Happy New Year 1

Calligraphy - Happy Birthday and Happy Easter in four styles (choose the style to suit your painting) 1 - standard, 2 - cursive, 3 - Han official, 4 - Qin Zhuan (ancient)

Happy Birthday

1

2

3

4

Happy Easter 2

Happy Easter

1

3

4

21

# Working with Other Shapes

## Fan aperture.

Cut-outs can be made to a variety of shapes and these are fun to experiment with. The composition in a fan shape will need careful thought, and again it is essential not to overcrowd the work. This shape is dealt with in more detail in the fan-making section.

## Multi apertures.

These can be in several designs, the most common one being the screen. This can be treated either as individual pictures, or a painting which goes right the way across. The example shown is a four-fold screen.

*Screen card which can be folded in half or zig-zag fashion into four. The mount can be a colour to suit the painting or as in this case brown to simulate wood. The painting is on silk acetate ribbon and continues behind the mount.*

The work can be done directly onto the card, or the apertures can be cut out and a paper or fabric painting placed behind. In the latter case a thin sheet of paper right across the back of the whole screen will neaten it and provide a message area.

## Irregular apertures.

There is no reason why designs cannot be done for any shape or size of aperture. As long as there is an appropriate amount of space a Chinese style painting will look fine. There are obviously certain shapes which are more suitable or more traditional, the long, narrow rectangle being one of them.

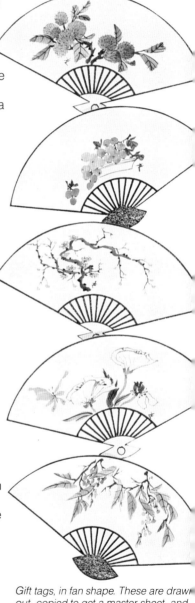

*Gift tags, in fan shape. These are drawn out, copied to get a master sheet, and then photocopied onto card. The blank tags can then be painted. Card is not so absorbent as paper.*

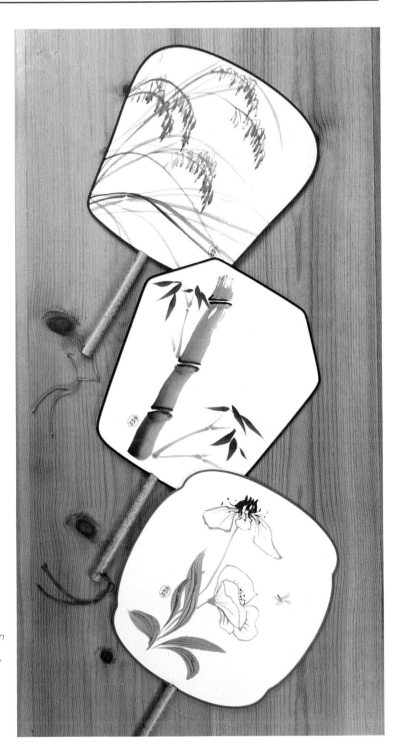

The rigid wire fans used to have tightly stretched silk paintings (tourist variety) across the frame. These had rotted but the frames were saved. They have been painted with Craft Colours and colour co-ordinated paintings mounted on the back. (When thoroughly dry, the painting can be lightly sprayed with clean water and left to dry naturally to flatten it). The fan is roughly cut to shape and then finally trimmed after fixing.

*Calligraphy - Best Wishes and Good Luck in four styles (choose the style to suit your painting)*
*1 - standard, 2 - cursive, 3 - Han official, 4 - Qin Zhuan (ancient)*

1

2

3

Best Wishes

1

2

3

4

Good Luck

Best Wishes 4

*Calligraphy - Bon Voyage and Get Well Soon in four styles (choose the style to suit your painting)*
*1 - standard, 2 - cursive, 3 - Han official, 4 - Qin Zhuan (ancient)*

Bon Voyage

1

2

3

4

Get Well Soon 1

Get Well Soon

2

3

4

25

# Bookmarks

These can be done in two ways. The first is to use a card mount as with the greetings cards. The aperture will therefore be long and narrow. Suitable designs could be landscapes, trailing plants or maybe a monkey hanging from a branch. Experiment to find out what fits and what you are happy with. The second method is to use some 'silk' ribbon with a fused edge (make sure that it is not a waterproof variety or it will not take the paint), carry out your design, and when dry place it between two layers of clear, adhesive film (the type used for protecting books), covering first one side and then the other.

# Calendars

These are treated in exactly the same way as the greetings cards. Usually they are sold with an envelope, often from photographic suppliers. The artwork is simply eased in from one side. The main thing to make note of here is the choice of design. A card can be removed from display at any time, but a calendar is likely to be in a prominent place all year. Do choose your subject with care!

# Gift tags

These can be painted on any shape. A fan shape is very pretty and some examples are shown among the illustrations.

*Dark coloured gift tags are striking if painted in white or pastel colours. Gold and silver can also be used.*

# Alternative Ideas for Cards

There are two other ideas for greetings cards that should be included here. One is the use of blank card which is then painted. This can be of any shape or size, but obviously the larger the painting then the more difficult it will be for the brush stroke to look right. If desired, an outline can be photocopied onto the card to 'frame' the painting, or some calligraphy can be included.

Another idea is to carry out a design, and then to have it copied, giving multiple copies. Of course this will only give tones of black and grey, so care will be needed to make these show up. Surface colouring can be done afterwards - this should be limited due to the time factor (if you spend a long time on this then it would be better to paint them all by hand!)

Colour copies can be obtained, but you would need to investigate the costings. Multiple cards are generally used for Christmas or for money-raising activities.

*Bookmarks in two styles. One method uses a card mount as in the greeting cards, the other has book film on both sides of the ribbon. All of these are painted on silk acetate ribbon.*

*The Osmiroid Christmas card for 1989 - colour copy of the original painting, produced in bulk.*

# Other Small Paintings

There are many small frames available and these all employ the techniques discussed previously for greetings cards. Small paintings can also be applied to keyrings, pendants and other jewellery, which are really miniatures and need a lot of care. The brush strokes should always be made properly and you should avoid going back over a stroke in the same way as with a larger work.

# Personal Stationery

Appropriately sized pieces of card may be decorated with a painting in one corner, or sheets of paper similarly dealt with could be used for correspondence cards or notepaper. Many different coloured papers and envelopes are available - again you will need a drier brush.

*Attractive notelets can be produced to add a personal touch to 'thank you' notes. These are painted on cards bought 'by the pound' with matching envelopes.*

*Multiple cards produced by reduction and copying onto card. The plum blossom and robins have limited colouring, the penguins are a straight photocopy. Use of a chop or seal on the back, or your signature etc. will add to the effect. The seal used on the reverse of the penguins says 'Seven Brush Strokes Studio'. The seals on the others are the Author's name in various styles. The envelope size should be considered when painting the cards - ideally it should be A4 or A5 folded in half in either direction.*

MERRY CHRISTMAS

we
wish
you a
joyous
Christmas

MERRY CHRISTMAS

# Making Fans

The fan shape has been dealt with, both for painting within the outline, and placing a painting behind the appropriate shape. Other variations are to use a rigid fan shape which has been made of bamboo or other wood. Sometimes these are available very cheaply with a printed picture on the back, which can be removed and replaced with your own work. These can look extremely pretty when hung in a window so that the light shows through and accentuates the colours and the transparency of the watercolour paints.

The other option is to use a fan 'blank' - the bamboo sticks of a folding fan. Using a suitable outline as a guide, the fan can be painted and fastened onto the sticks. There are two ways of doing this.

The first is to find a cheap printed fan, and remove the paper by soaking. When dry, the paper can be used as a pattern to cut out your own design. Care must be taken to stick it onto the bamboo in the same manner as the original.

The second method is to buy the bare sticks and to make the fan using two layers. After the painting has been completed on the fan shape, it is glued to another piece of paper (which may be decorated or plain), but with pockets left so that the sticks may be slid into the spaces. This is achieved by glueing only along the folds. After the sticks have been slid into place a small amount of glue on each stick will hold it firmly. If several of these are made, a template could be produced to speed up the glueing process. Folding of the paper in either of these methods should be carried out with care and neatness, keeping the folds evenly spaced.

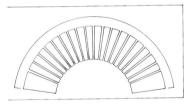

*To help with making a fan, cut out a template from a piece of card. Most fans have 16, 17 or 18 sticks. Mark off on both the inner and outer edges into equal segments - this will assist with both the positioning of the sticks and the folding.*

*For the 'pocket' method, another template can be made where holes are cut into the card where the paste is required. Tolerance is required as the paste can spread a little when the two papers are put together.*

# Presentation

With any work you do, after putting the time and effort into carrying it out, you should be conscious of the final appearance. Try to keep things clean, make sure any seals or labels are put on straight and, if selling, put your cards into clear plastic envelopes.

*Three folding fans produced by different methods.*

*This is the simplest technique. The fan shape is painted with a suitable design On the back the folds are marked on lightly with pencil and folded. The sticks are then glued (with a paper adhesive) to alternate folds. The outer sticks are attached, one in front and one behind. Make sure that you have it the correct way (this applies to all the fans) - the top stick is to the right and the underneath one to the left.*

*The second method is to lightly mark the positions of the sticks onto a plain piece of paper and glue them in place. Carefully paste the paper and lower the painting on top of the sticks. Positioning should be with care. Leave to dry and then cut to shape - it is easier to cut the inner edge before gluing and take extra care on the position of both papers when sticking them together. The folds can now be done.*

*The third fan is made by gluing along the top of the fan and down between the stick positions. The two pieces of paper are placed together and left to dry. Final trimming is carried out and the folds put in. The sticks are then eased into the pockets and the end sticks glued into place. It will help to start at one end and to have the folds close together. Try not to bend the stick too much as they may snap off.*

# AROUND THE HOME

Apart from the framed or mounted picture, which is frequently used to decorate the home or other environment, there are several other ideas that can be explored. For example, a painting, either on paper or silk, could be placed behind another surface. The following are some examples - you may be able to think of others.

# Paperweights

These can be readily obtained from craft and art outlets, or by mail order. They can be of varying sizes and weights. Try to use a subject that suits the shape. Material such as silk can look very beautiful as the glass will magnify the thread pattern. Choose a design that will suit the surroundings.

Once the painting has been done, cut neatly round the shape. Most manufacturers supply a flock backing which is self-adhesive. Place the design carefully, check if any packing is required (card or tissue), and then stick the backing into place. Again it is important to be neat and tidy. This will show care and will be appreciated.

Handle silk and other materials carefully, otherwise fraying will occur. One technique which can be used to avoid this is to spray a piece of paper or thin card with a fine adhesive before placing the painting gently on top, and then cutting round the design when dry.

*Paperweights and coaster all on 'silk' ribbon.*

# Glass Coasters

These are often available from the same outlets as the paperweights and are treated in the same way. if a set is to be made, then make sure that the background is the same colour for all. These can also be used as trinket trays.

# Fingerplates & Lightswitch Covers

These are readily available from hardware shops and are made of clear plastic. Once again the design is painted and attached to the back of the plate with a small amount of adhesive to prevent movement. The fingerplate is then screwed to the door using the holes provided.

Lightswitch covers are also available in the same material and you could co-ordinate the paintings. Subjects suitable for the room can be chosen: fish for the bathroom, vegetables for the kitchen, flowers for a bedroom (colour co-ordinated of course), and amusing animals for a child's room.

In a modern home the emphasis might be on the stark and simple, whereas in a cottage the choice could be more full and pretty.

*Door fingerplates - suitable for perhaps bedroom and a bathroom. This one has been painted on paper.*

*Lightswitch covers - the frogs would be fun for a child's room.*

33

Any iced cake can be decorated. This one is for a Golden Wedding Anniversary, but could easily be for a birthday as well. The cake band and card are all matching. You could carry the theme further by painting matching napkin rings and painting a flower on the serviettes (very dry brush).

More examples of cake bands - the fish would delight a child, the convulvulus would be pretty for birthday or Mother's Day cake, and the poinsettia is an obvious choice for Christmas. These are all on silk acetate ribbon with a fused edge.

A tray, chopping bat and cheese board are some of the ideas for laminating your paintings onto useful items. The mats at the beginning of this chapter are also laminated. Silk or cotton can be used but some of the other fabrics do not stand the heat required for lamination. As with the coasters, if making a set then make sure that the backgrounds match. Also beware of some of the papers - the paper used for these examples was handmade and the fibres showed up far more after lamination than before. Designs for a set of mats for example can be all different, or varying paintings of the same flower.

# Memo Holders and Napkin Rings

Memo holders are available in plastic form to take small paintings. The size of the design is marked out, painted, and then pushed into the slot.

Temporary napkin rings can be made by following the bookmark principle, using book covering film, but joining the two ends together by overlapping the plastic film. You could do a special design to fit in with the table decor or something appropriate to the occasion.

Books, albums and folders can be decorated, again using a painting and the clear book film. Care must be taken to get the design straight and to cut off any fraying which may occur.

# Cake Decorating

Using food colouring and *clean* brushes, the top and sides of an iced cake can be painted. Choose an appropriate subject. Christmas time could mean pine branches, poinsettia or holly; a wedding anniversary might involve flowers of the appropriate colour, or symbolism such as a pair of mandarin ducks. The colours do give a transparent effect, rather like watercolours.

To complete the design, or as a separate idea, you could use a piece of ribbon as a cake frill, again decorated with a suitable design. A piece of bookfilm on the back would prevent any grease seeping through from the cake or decorations. This idea can be used for even a simple sponge to make it a beautiful gift.

*A plastic memo holder for holding note on the fridge etc. The paper painting is simply pushed in between the two surfaces.*

*Napkin rings can be purchased or made. These examples use bookfilm to cover and join the length of ribbon. A red napkin with poinsettias for Christmas, blue with summer flowers for a birthday or anniversary.*

# PAINTING ON FABRIC

The irises are painted up from the waist - if tucking this tee shirt into skirt or trousers, then work out where the design needs to start. The dragonfly forms a large part of this composition. This teeshirt is of thicker quality.

The red teeshirt was painted with main Craft Colours as these are more opaque and therefore show up against the darker fabric. Again the insect gives a more lively design.

Red/orange flowers painted down from the shoulder. Painted in the usual order of petals, leaves, stem and detail. The insect adds some humour to the composition. General fabric paints were used for this one and the irises.

*Illustrated overleaf is a fine silk scarf with rolled edges. It shows both outline and solid strokes and was painted with silk paints.*

The cushion was painted on upholstery
fabric which has a rich, silky sheen.
Part of the meilin orchid could be three-
dimensional if desired, or top stitching
introduced for effect.

All the painting techniques that have been introduced can be applied to painting on fabric. How to paint a card or bookmark using a piece of silk or other fabric with watercolour paints is covered in the earlier chapter. When a larger work is required, such as a picture, the silk can be stretched on a frame and sized with alum solution, or you can buy ready-sized painting silk. It can also be obtained mounted onto paper. Whichever type you use, you will find that a drier brush is more successful. You can avoid sizing the silk if you work with a brush in one hand and a hair-drier in the other!

To paint on a piece of fabric for dressmaking or on a ready-made article of clothing needs different methods and materials. As the item will be worn, laundering. or at least sponging must be possible, and therefore special paints will be required. Many types are available; some especially for silk, others for more general use. It will be easier to use the various examples as illustration.

# Tee-Shirts

Most fabric paints can also be used for stencilling and printing. This book deals only with painting in the Chinese style.

It is always best to first wash the item to be decorated. This will remove any dressing that may have been used. Place a piece of card or a pad of newspaper inside the tee-shirt to prevent the paint seeping through, and anchor with weights or sticky tape onto a flat surface.

Mix or shake the paint thoroughly. Most fabric paints can be diluted with water and changed to pastel shades with white. Blend the paints and apply them as if painting on paper, but using a slightly drier brush. The amount of liquid will depend on the quality and composition of the shirt, more pressure and a slower stroke may be required to allow the paint to be absorbed, but do not allow the paint to continue spreading too far. The advantage of painting in this style on a tee-shirt is that the techniques for blending and loading the colour on the brush cannot be carried out by commercial printing, so aim for strokes which make full use of variation in colour.

When the design is completed (remember that space is important) it should be hung in a warm atmosphere to dry completely. Drying can be accelerated with a hairdryer. The colour is then fixed by ironing. The work should be covered with thin cotton and the iron used on a cotton setting for about one minute, moving the iron the whole time to avoid any risk of scorching.

There are a few paints available for use on both fabric and pottery - the Osmiroid Craft Colours for example.

This book does not deal with alcohol-based paints. These are fixed by steaming which is a far more involved process. With all types of paint the manufacturer's instructions should be carefully followed.

Reactive cold dyes can be used for painting. In this technique, the fabric is dipped in warm water with 10 grams/1 litre of soda ash (washing soda). The material is dried and ironed flat.

The dye powder is then dissolved in water (½ spoonful in 50ml water will give a strong colour), and used in the usual way. A thickener can be added to slow down the spread of paint into the fabric. Dry and iron as before.

The excess dye has then to be removed by washing with a small amount of detergent, keeping the material moving in the water to prevent any colour going where it should not! Rinse, dry and iron flat.

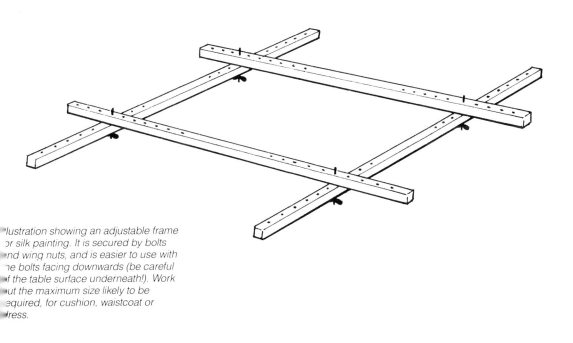

*Illustration showing an adjustable frame for silk painting. It is secured by bolts and wing nuts, and is easier to use with the bolts facing downwards (be careful of the table surface underneath!). Work out the maximum size likely to be required, for cushion, waistcoat or dress.*

*Silk painting samplers, showing the two main techniques and their application to Chinese Brush Painting. All are on very fine silk which was washed before painting; the paints are specifically for silk.*

*The first uses gutta to outline the design, and areas are then filled in with colour. This method, apart from being able to use Chinese subjects, did not seem to have much affinity to the usual brush strokes.*

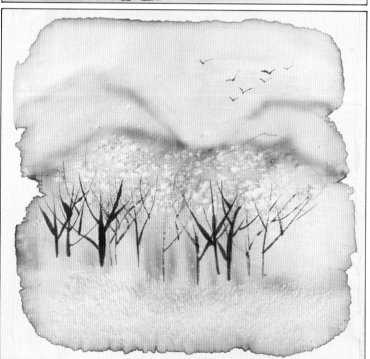

*The second is a very free style, with the paint being allowed to go into the silk as far as it wishes, even being 'assisted' with some extra water in places. Control over the amount of liquid in the brush is very important here. The fine detail work had the hairdrier running while the strokes were made. The shimmer on the water and the blossom were created by using salt. Very dry strokes across the sky added another effect.*

Thirdly, a very traditional painting of a single lotus. The silk sheen on the leaf is very attractive, and the darker paint on the tip of the brush has added to the effect.

The landscape was a mixture of freeflowing and controlled strokes. The lake in the distance had additional water added to give a pale horizon. With all the designs, some idea of the final effect required is necessary.

# Silk Scarves

Both of the above types of paint can be used for silk (use 5 grams of soda ash to prepare the fabric for the dyes instead of 10 grams). However there are many products on the market which although primarily intended for use with silk can also be used on other materials including cotton. It would be best to select one which suits your choice of work.

For a scarf you will need a frame of adequate size. The silk has to be suspended to prevent the paint running too far. The frame can be an old picture frame, homemade, or a purchased, adjustable type. For experimenting a picture frame would be quite sufficient. (For small pieces, an embroidery frame can be used, or even an elastic band spread over the top of a jam jar!)

A scarf will tend to be made from a fine piece of silk. The rougher types of silk will not allow smooth brush strokes. Remember to allow enough material to turn a rolled hem. The finished size of the scarf should be about 665mm square (26"). Wash the silk in hand-hot water and iron while damp. Secure the silk to the frame with pins (a three pronged variety is available for this purpose). On one side put pins in each corner and the centre, then place more pins at 50mm (2") intervals between the first three. Treat the other sides in the same manner. Prop the frame on blocks or pieces of wood to raise it off the table surface. The frame may be protected by waterproof adhesive tape if you wish.

There are two main techniques for this stage. One is to allow the colours to mingle and blend, sometimes even giving them a helping hand by adding water after the paint has been applied to the silk. The other is to outline the design with gutta (a product giving a colourless line; the gutta is removed by washing prior to fixing), before applying the other colours - this will limit the colours into definite areas and give a more precise design. Salt (cooking, water softener type or special effect salt) can also be used to give interesting, but unpredictable results. It works by drying up the liquid and therefore taking the colour out where it touches. This can be in dots or more irregular shapes as the salt is moved around. It is left on the silk until the fabric is dry and then brushed off.

Either work directly onto the silk, or have a rough sketch and place it underneath so that it can be seen through the fabric (if using the outline technique, be careful that the wet gutta does not stick to the paper pattern). Choose one technique, or maybe a mixture of the two. If the silk is drying too quickly then it should be wetted with clean water before applying the paint. To add detail such as veins on leaves, then have a hairdryer running and play it on the surface of the fabric while you are painting - this stage must

*Small fabric scroll painted with watercolour onto the 'silk' ribbon with a fused edge. The ends have then been wrapped around pieces of dowel to imitate a scroll.*

be done when the rest is dry. When you wash your brush out to change the colour, dry the brush on a tissue before picking up more paint, rather than dilute the next brush load. This also prevents the colour spreading further than required.

While the work is finally drying, wash out the brushes carefully. Then iron the silk to fix the colours, if this is the recommended technique for the paint - some use a fixative which has to be painted on. The scarf is now ready to be hemmed. If making a shawl, follow the same instructions, using a square piece of material 975mm - 1125mm (38'' - 45'').

This method can also be used to make greeting cards, but does involve far more work than the previous techniques.

# Silk Waistcoat or Blouse

This follows all the previous stages. You will need a large frame, and there will not be the opportunity to cut the silk economically. Any spare material may be decorated and used to make up a small purse to match the garment. The pattern piece can be marked out in pencil so that the design is in the correct place. It is best to mark the outer edge of the seam so that there is no chance of the marks showing at the end. Collars, cuffs and pockets can also be decorated.

A readymade garment could be used, but care is required to protect the rest of the material.

# Fabric Scroll

This can be done using the above techniques, or, as it does not have to be washed, can be painted in watercolours. The edge needs to be fused though, and so a length of ribbon is rather better for this than a cut piece of fabric. Cut two pieces of dowel, allowing 6mm (½'') extra each side, and glue the fabric to the dowel with clear adhesive. Neatness is essential. Make sure that you allow the material to hang straight. It is advisable to cut it generously so that the fabric can go round the dowel a few times. The ends of the dowel can be painted or covered in tape if required.

*Another small scroll, this time it has been slotted into slits in the card backing and secured at the back. The water on the waterfall has been emphasised by painting the rest of the ribbon with cold tea!*

Blouse in a heavier weight of silk. It was marked out, painted, and then cut and made up. Silk paints were used. The wisteria design makes good use of the shape and hanging nature of the plant.

The lampshade was painted with a mixture of fabric paints, while on a frame. The bauhinia flowers will suit a variety of situations. With a painted shade, a plain lampbase is necessary, or maybe with a single related flower. The shade was made using a piece of celluloid for stiffening so that the transparent effect is maximised with the light switched on. A simple band of ribbon was used to finish off the top and bottom.

# Lampshades

Again these can be painted in watercolour, but it is often an advantage to be able to sponge off any marks. You can either use a readymade lampshade, or decorate the fabric and then assemble the shade. It is obviously best not to use a shade with a lot of pleats or gathers.

*This fan was produced very simply! It was purchased with a plain material attached (variety unknown). Unlike watercolours, the fabric paints penetra through the fabric and so the design was painted on the back and the completed fan turned over.*

# Cushions

These can be single or double sided. As they take quite a lot of stress, a heavier silk will be necessary, unless the design is backed and quilted for example. As described elsewhere, additional pieces may be added for interest, but, as with all your designs, beware of adding too much and losing the simple Chinese style. If the design is only required on one side, use a toning colour (or the same plain fabric) for the back - again this will add the impression of more space. Any shape can be made - it is up to you!

# Fans

As described before, there are many designs for these. With the rigid frame variety, silk can be used together with the fabric paints. Again neat finishing off is necessary, especially if the fan is to be hung in a window where the back may be seen. A thin paper lining could be used to protect and neaten the back if required.

*Rigid bamboo fan. This example has a paper backing but could easily be fabric. The frame was originally purchased with a mass-produced painting on it.*

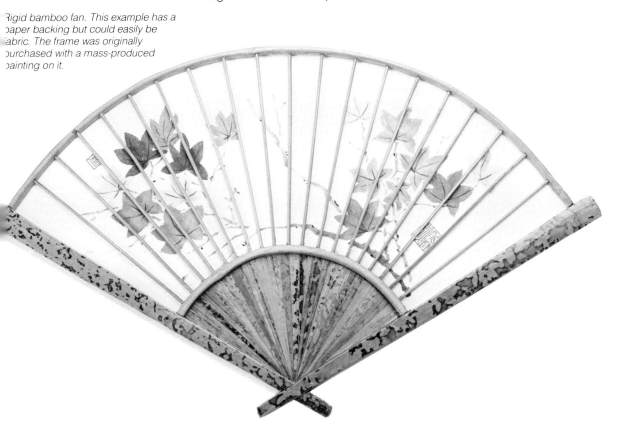

Opposite page shows the 'dragon
chasing pearls of wisdom' design on
this waistcoat gives an exotic touch to a
plain garment. The heavier weight of
silk was used together with silk paints.

roses as painted on the teashirt on page
8.

In the style of the oriental table lamps, a wooden frame can be made up as the illustration, incorporating a bulb holder in the base. The height can be 400 - 500mm and the sides 120 - 180mm wide. Painted panels of fabric or paper can be glued to the inside of the frame so that the light shines through. Do make sure that there is no danger of the bulb touching or scorching the sides. A 60 watt bulb should be bright enough.

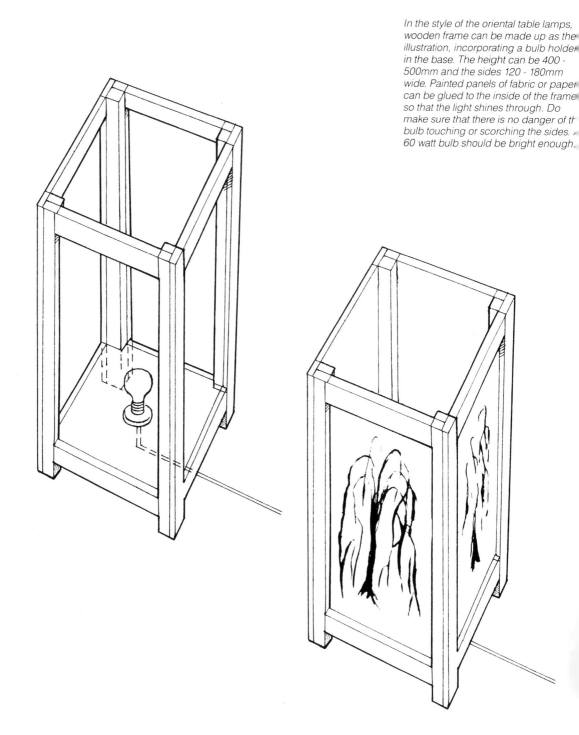

# PAINTING ON POTTERY

The picture overleaf shows a tile which was been framed. Underglaze paints were used with a clear glaze.

The wisteria lampbase makes full use of the graceful hanging nature of the plant. Each side was painted with due regard to the adjacent sides, the foliage linking the panels around the top. Again underglaze paints were used. The bees were added in overglaze paint when fingerprints appeared from the kiln loading - do make a mental note of where your signature is positioned! However they do add a lively touch to the lamp.

*Mugs, small jug and the ginger jar, all in underglaze colours. Do consider the shape of your pottery when choosing a subject to paint.*

This subject is obviously more specialised, but is perfectly possible. There are different ways in which it can be done depending on the facilities available.

# Using a Kiln

With this method you either have to know someone with a kiln who is willing to fire things for you, or to have your own. Sometimes a local school has spare capacity in the school kilns and will help you. Many potters already use Chinese brushes for painting on pottery, and others attend Chinese Brush Painting classes to learn the strokes for use on their own pots.

For pure decoration and with a means of firing, the following method should be used. The selected article, which could be a jug, vase or lamp base should be purchased readymade or moulded from clay slip. The pottery will be in the biscuit state (ie. after the first firing).

Use a 2H pencil to sketch on the design, but be careful to keep plenty of space in the painting. The pencil marks will disappear when fired. The painting is done using underglaze paints and Chinese brushes. With red it is not so easy to get a smooth stroke, so it is best to avoid large areas of this colour. The modelling strokes on petals and leaves are used in the usual manner. Outline technique is particularly good. The pottery is very absorbent in a similar way to the paper, but it has one great advantage - you can sandpaper out your mistakes!

The pot is then glazed and fired in the normal way. If ready-glazed pottery is used, then onglaze paints are employed, however, these can create difficulties with large smooth strokes. Outline technique is probably the best to use. The pots are then fired again to fix the colours.

The colours of the underglaze and onglaze paints do change on firing, so make sure that you test them first.

*I am sad without you*

*Brush (for use on a painting with good strokes)*

## Using an Oven

There are paints available that can be used in conjunction with an ordinary domestic oven. They are applied as the paints onto ready-glazed pottery, and are then 'finished' in the oven. Again the better technique would be to use small or outline strokes.

*Member of the Chinese Brush Painters Society*

## Designing for Pottery

In deciding on designs for rounded items such as ginger jars and milk jugs, careful consideration should be given to the subject that you wish to paint. For a jug it may be an idea to use a fish, allowing the tail to flow towards the spout. For a rounded vase the design will look better if it flows around the pot. A square lamp base, for example, could either have the pattern flowing round from one side to another, or a different design on each side. It will always look better if the designs are related and perhaps within the same colour theme.

*Ink (for use with satisfactory ink tones)*

*Autumn*

*All things in nature are beautiful.*

*There is never a day when I do nothing.*

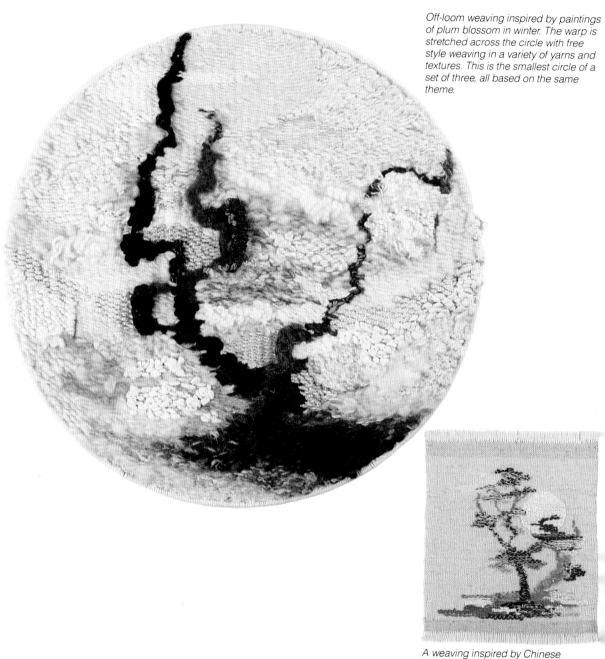

*Off-loom weaving inspired by paintings of plum blossom in winter. The warp is stretched across the circle with free style weaving in a variety of yarns and textures. This is the smallest circle of a set of three, all based on the same theme.*

*A weaving inspired by Chinese paintings and landscapes. Woven on a four shaft loom using Moorman technique. This method is very pictorial and the pattern only occurs on the one side of the fabric.*

# INSPIRATION
# USING CHINESE
# PAINTING

The simplicity and imagery of Chinese Brush Painting can be used as an inspiration for many other art forms and crafts. It can be used to illustrate fashion designs, for designing embroidery patterns, for weaving, knitting and so on. Chinese symbolism can be used for any decoration which will introduce interesting effects.

Try out ideas either using the Chinese Brush Painting as a means of formulating and illustrating those ideas, or use the painting method to actually carry out the work. The spacial concept can be very welcome after some of the fashions for very intricate patterns. The contast between the two styles can add interest and excitement.

The use of simple areas of colour, like brush strokes, in a fabric or paper collage can be most effective. As mentioned in the fabric painting chapter, a design can be used for a cushion with embroidery on the surface; additional small padded pieces can be made and then attached. For example, a group of flower stems could be painted and top stitched with machine or embroidery stitches. One of the flowers could be repeated on a separate piece of fabric, then backed, padded and attached over the top of the other flower to give a three-dimensional design. These ideas can be adapted to your own techniques and abilities.

Having tried Chinese Brush Painting, and hopefully carried out some of the exercises in this book, you will find that there are many ways in which this style of art can be applied to existing craft techniques, or to open up a whole new range of activities.

*An associated art form in China is papercutting. This dramatic card incorporates calligraphy and papercutting, using the same type of mount as the painted cards.*

*All flowers bloom together*

*Friends of mankind (for use on an animal painting)*

*The sky is so high, birds fly where they wish.*

*Fish's happiness (from a Chinese story).*

*Overleaf shows another Moorman weaving inspired by Chinese art.*

*All the characters used on the seals are from very ancient scripts. They were carved by Qu Lei Lei.*

Calligraphy - Happy Anniversary,
Golden and Silver in four styles (choose
the style to suit your painting)
1 - standard, 2 - cursive, 3 - Han official,
4 - Qin Zhuan (ancient)

Happy Anniversary

1

2

4

Happy Anniversary 3

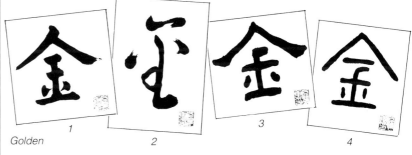

Golden

1

2

3

4

Silver

1

2

3

4

# Osmiroid Creative Leisure Series

Each title in the Osmiroid Creative Leisure series has been written in a lively "to the point" style, with very practical advice to ensure that exciting creative results are quickly achievable.

**Colour Calligraphy** explains colour theory and shows some of the many ways that imaginative colour calligraphy can be created.

**Pen and Ink Drawing** leads the reader through many subjects and styles and includes enough "tricks of the trade" to ensure that everyone can create something.

**The Art of Sketching** shows the reader how to approach sketching from a very practical viewpoint, covering a wide range of indoor and outdoor subjects.

**The Art of Poster Making** shows the reader how to create posters using the wide variety of media and ideas.

**The Art of Stencilling** gives the reader all they need to know to stencil onto walls, fabrics, furniture or paper, with manufactured or home made stencils.

## Acknowledgements

Grateful thanks to Qu Lei Lei for permission to use his work, to Tess, Jackie and Barbara for lending the wisteria lamp, panda painting and their help, also special thanks to my husband David for his patience! Lamination of mats, tray and cheeseboards by Locality Arts Ltd., Coign House, Wicklewood, Wymondham, Norfolk.

Design and artwork by Nigel Long, Winchester